TWO SKELETONS ON THE TELEPHONE

Poems
by
Paul Duggan

Pictures
by
Daniel Sylvestre

AND OTHER POEMS FROM TOUGH CITY

The Millbrook Press   Brookfield, Connecticut

First published in Canada under the title
MURPHY THE RAT AND OTHER TALES OF TOUGH CITY
Red Deer College Press

First published in the United States in 1999
by The Millbrook Press, Inc.
2 Old New Milford Road
Brookfield, Connecticut 06804
Visit us at our Web site — http://www.millbrookpress.com

Published by arrangement with Northern Lights
Books for Children, Red Deer College Press
Red Deer, Alberta, Canada

Library of Congress Cataloging-in-Publication Data
Duggan, Paul.
[Murphy the Rat and other tales of Tough City]
Two skeletons on the telephone and other poems from Tough City/
poems by Paul Duggan; pictures by Daniel Sylvestre.
p. cm.
"First published in Canada under the title: Murphy the Rat and other tales of Tough City"—T.p. verso.
Summary: A collection of poems with an emphasis on the grisly or ghastly, including "If Your're Strolling
in a Sewer," "Mr. One Leg," and "A Vampire Bit a Ghostly Neck."
ISBN 0-7613-1451-2 (lib. bdg.)
1. Horror Juvenile poetry. 2. Halloween Juvenile poetry. 3. Children's poetry, Canadian. [1. Horror Poetry.
2. Humorous poetry. 3. Canadian poetry.] I. Sylvestre, Daniel, ill. II. Title.
PR9199.3.D837M87   1999
811'.54—dc21   99-20022   CIP

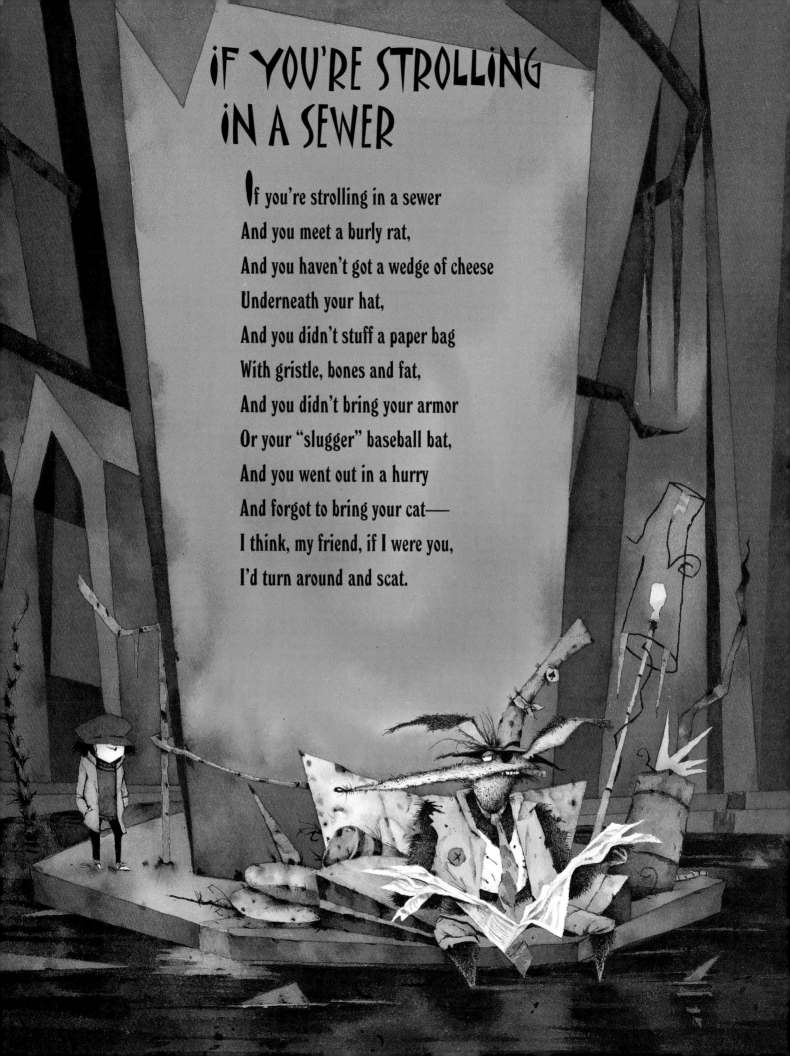

iF YOU'RE STROLLING IN A SEWER

If you're strolling in a sewer
And you meet a burly rat,
And you haven't got a wedge of cheese
Underneath your hat,
And you didn't stuff a paper bag
With gristle, bones and fat,
And you didn't bring your armor
Or your "slugger" baseball bat,
And you went out in a hurry
And forgot to bring your cat—
I think, my friend, if I were you,
I'd turn around and scat.

MURPHY THE RAT

Murphy in a scrap is vicious and mean,

His long yellow teeth are the sharpest I've seen.

He was born in the sewers under Tough City

And goes looking for fights calling, "Here Kitty, Kitty!"

BUGGED

A drive in the moonlight's a tonic to me,
I love every sound, every sight;
Except for those streaks on the windshield you see—
From things that go splat in the night.

MR. ONE LEG

Sal met a man with only one leg,
And she didn't mean to stare,
But he had no head, no body at all—
There was only one leg standing there.

THE BARLEY BOYS

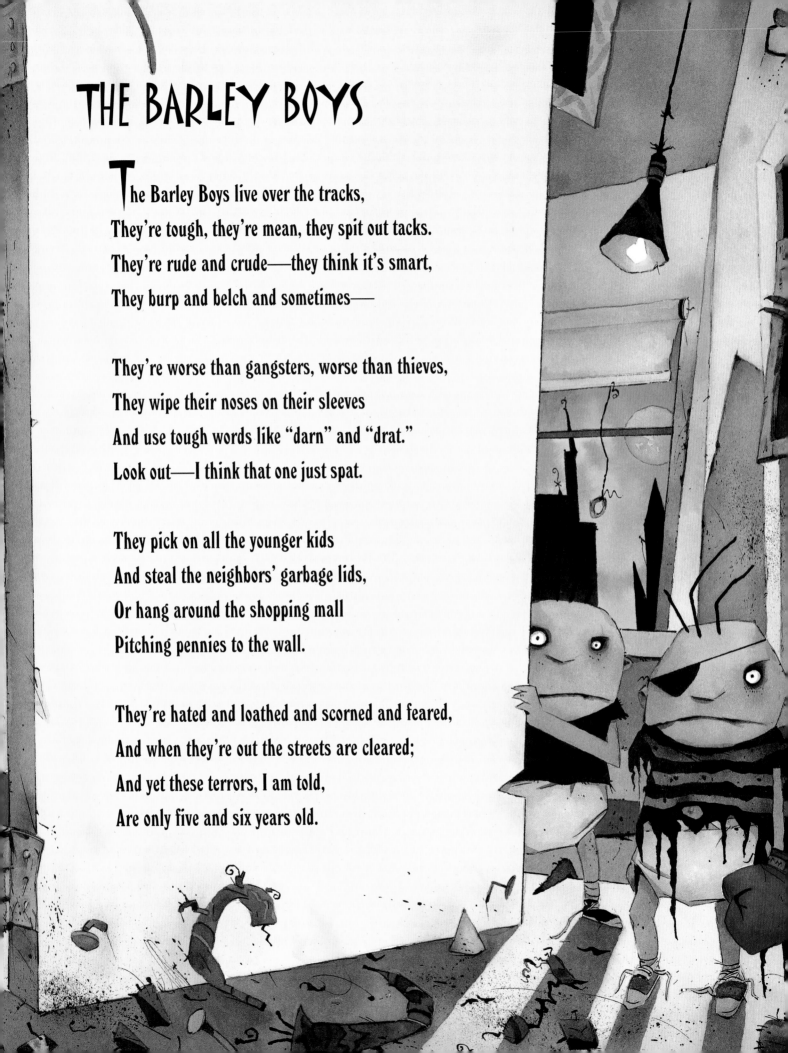

The Barley Boys live over the tracks,
They're tough, they're mean, they spit out tacks.
They're rude and crude—they think it's smart,
They burp and belch and sometimes—

They're worse than gangsters, worse than thieves,
They wipe their noses on their sleeves
And use tough words like "darn" and "drat."
Look out—I think that one just spat.

They pick on all the younger kids
And steal the neighbors' garbage lids,
Or hang around the shopping mall
Pitching pennies to the wall.

They're hated and loathed and scorned and feared,
And when they're out the streets are cleared;
And yet these terrors, I am told,
Are only five and six years old.

OH, HOW STRANGE

Oh, how strange is my Uncle Ned!

He wears a cat on his balding head.

When asked why he wears a cat for a wig,

He says that he sneezes when wearing a pig.

MORRIS FLETT

I knew a fellow named Morris Flett,

He jumped in the ocean but he didn't get wet;

He jumped on a griddle but he didn't get burned,

He jumped to the moon and he never returned.

THE RAT CATCHER

The rat catcher who tried
To catch Murphy the Rat
Is a fellow who's easy to spot;
He walks around with one leg in a cast,
The other leg tied in a knot.
His shirt is in shreds,
Like it's been through the wars,
And each ear is a black-and-blue lump;
And he always stands
With his back to the wall—
For his pants are chewed through
At the rump.

THE GHOUL

The ghoul's a walking Book of Knowledge
On everything from boats to planes,
But did he learn by going to College?
No! By picking people's brains.

A VAMPIRE BIT A GHOSTLY NECK

A vampire bit a ghostly neck,
Which means it wasn't there;
And so the vampire ended up
Just sucking on thin air.

MURPHY'S FAVORITE SAYINGS

Murphy has a few sayings he loves to use,
Like "a stitch in time" or "tit for tat."
But the one that really expresses his views?
"There's more than one way to skin a cat."

THE REASON SKELETONS DON'T WEAR CLOTHES

The reason skeletons don't wear clothes?

Socks won't stay on bony toes,

And underwear just sags and slumps

When hanging from their bony rumps.

Shirts slide off their bony backs,

And pants drop like potato sacks;

And since they can't wear fancy stuff,

Skeletons walk 'round in the buff.

UNCLE NED

They played a trick on Uncle Ned,
It made the neighbors grin,
They pumped him full of helium—
Then poked him with a pin.

THERE'S A THING

There's a Thing that's waiting outside my door—
I gave it candy, it wanted more.
I gave it a bagful, then two, then three,
But it won't go away—I think it wants me.

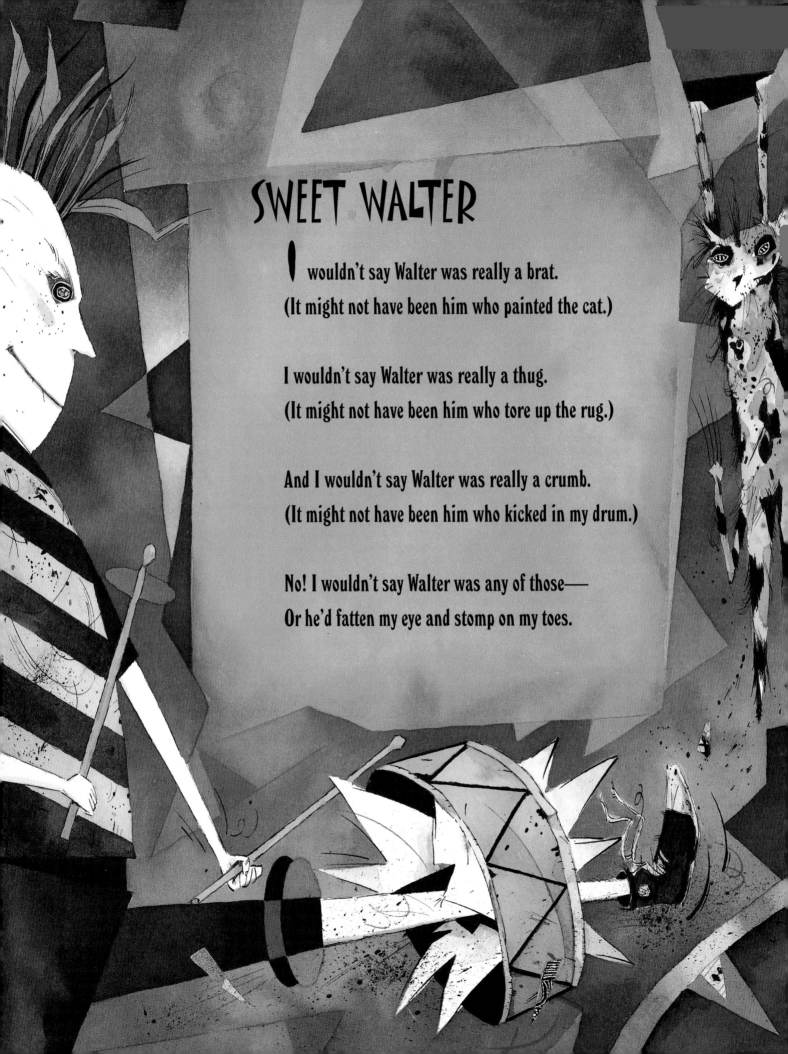

SWEET WALTER

I wouldn't say Walter was really a brat.
(It might not have been him who painted the cat.)

I wouldn't say Walter was really a thug.
(It might not have been him who tore up the rug.)

And I wouldn't say Walter was really a crumb.
(It might not have been him who kicked in my drum.)

No! I wouldn't say Walter was any of those—
Or he'd fatten my eye and stomp on my toes.

WEREWOLVES

If there are no such things as werewolves
When the moon is full and round,
Why is Philip growing hairy?
And what's that O-O-O-O-O-I-N-G sound?
And why is brother Philip growing fangs and power jaws?
If there are no such things as werewolves,
Then how come he has claws?

SALLY, GO AND BRUSH YOUR TEETH

Sally, go and brush your teeth,
Brush them good and hard;
They look like they were left beneath
The compost in the yard.

THE LIVELY TRICK

Phil played a lively trick on Pop
While he was having a scrub;
Phil took a pair of alley cats
And dropped them in the tub.

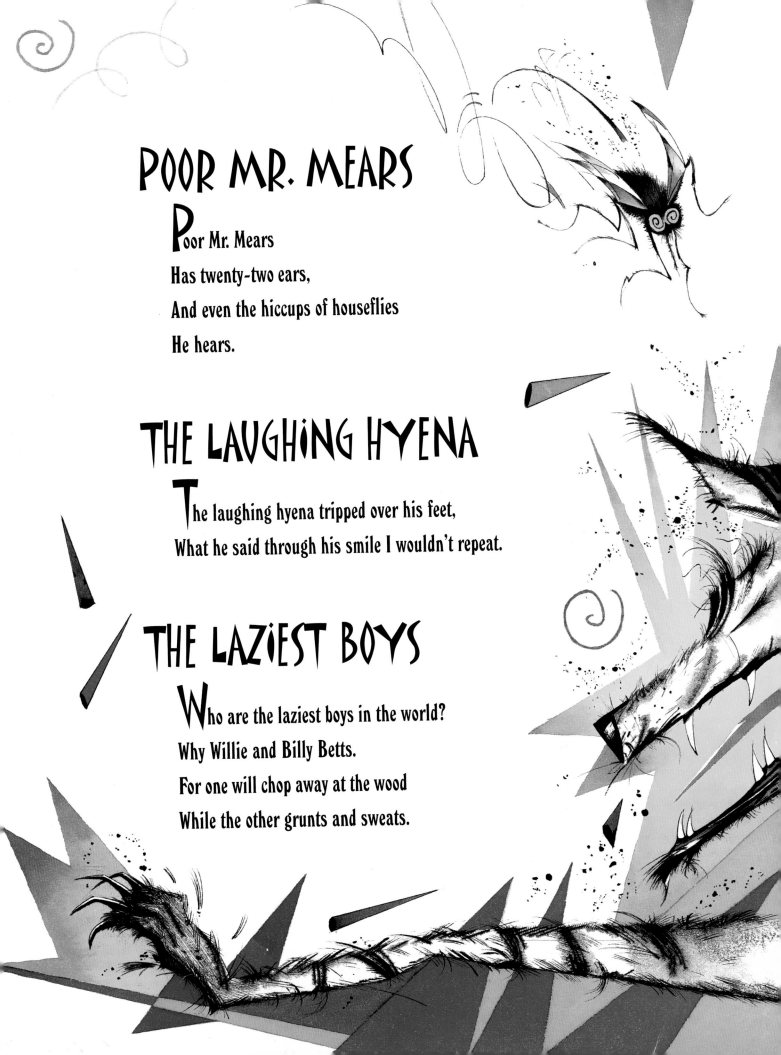

POOR MR. MEARS

Poor Mr. Mears
Has twenty-two ears,
And even the hiccups of houseflies
He hears.

THE LAUGHING HYENA

The laughing hyena tripped over his feet,
What he said through his smile I wouldn't repeat.

THE LAZIEST BOYS

Who are the laziest boys in the world?
Why Willie and Billy Betts.
For one will chop away at the wood
While the other grunts and sweats.

TWO SKELETONS ON THE TELEPHONE

Two skeletons on the telephone—
Nothing but idle chatter.
Hear their jaws go up and down,
Clatter! Clatter! Clatter!

Two skeletons on the telephone—
Yackety-yack all day.
Just a pair of empty heads
With nothing much to say.

i SAW A GHOST

I saw a ghost last Saturday night,
His arms were thin, his face was white;
He grinned at me and started to moan,
And in the blink of an eye
That ghost was alone.

DON'T WORRY

Don't worry if you catch a cold
And sneeze with might and main,
Dad says it's Mother Nature's way
Of dusting out the brain.

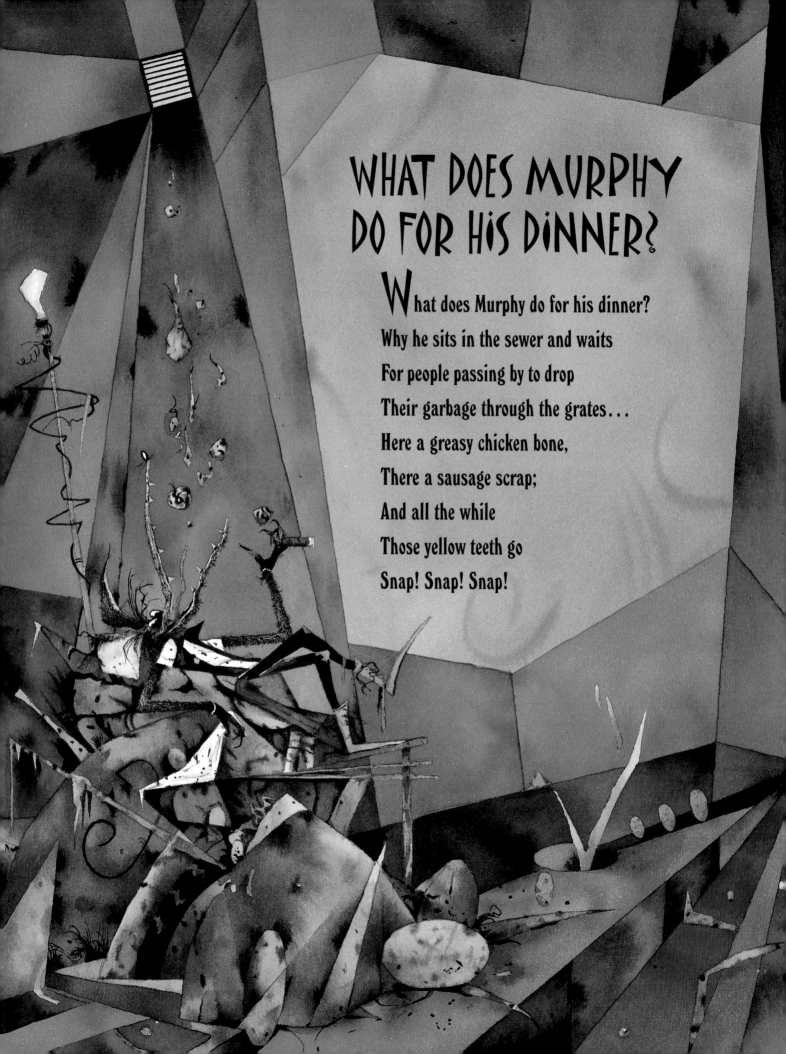

WHAT DOES MURPHY DO FOR HIS DINNER?

What does Murphy do for his dinner?

Why he sits in the sewer and waits

For people passing by to drop

Their garbage through the grates…

Here a greasy chicken bone,

There a sausage scrap;

And all the while

Those yellow teeth go

Snap! Snap! Snap!

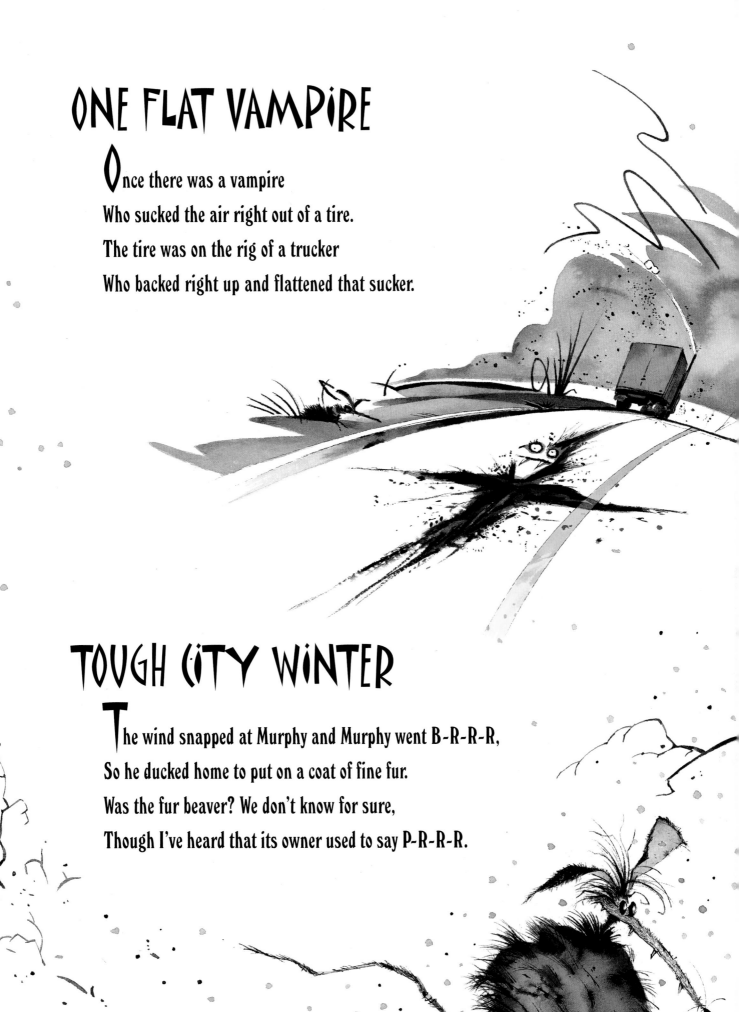

ONE FLAT VAMPIRE

Once there was a vampire
Who sucked the air right out of a tire.
The tire was on the rig of a trucker
Who backed right up and flattened that sucker.

TOUGH CITY WINTER

The wind snapped at Murphy and Murphy went B-R-R-R,
So he ducked home to put on a coat of fine fur.
Was the fur beaver? We don't know for sure,
Though I've heard that its owner used to say P-R-R-R.

SWEET WALTER IS EVER SO HELPFUL

Why is it when Walter smacks a mosquito
It's always on top of your head;
And you never ever feel a sting,
Just his walloping hand instead?

And why is it such a big favor
When he kicks you square in the pants?
He will modestly say he was just helping out
By booting a couple of ants.

Oh, Sweet Walter is ever so helpful,
He's a great friend to have, I suppose,
But watch that the bee that you never did see
Doesn't land on the tip of your nose.

REFLECTIONS

If you stand before a mirror
And give your hardest stare,
But see no one behind you—
That means a Vampire's there.

MORRIS THE FIREMAN

Morris may be a fireman,
But he's not like the other fellows;
While they take their hoses to three-alarm fires,
Morris takes marshmallows.

i ONCE HAD A GENIE

I once had a Genie trapped in a bottle
And hoped to use it for getting three wishes,
But my brother's one person I'd sure like to throttle—
For drowning that Genie while washing the dishes.

NORMAN'S BEARD

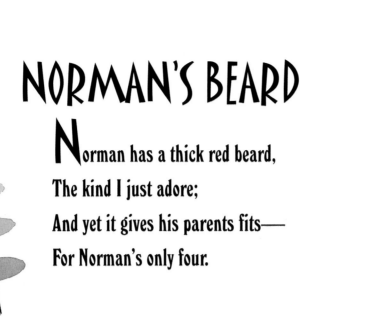

Norman has a thick red beard,
The kind I just adore;
And yet it gives his parents fits—
For Norman's only four.

THE TOE-PLUCKER

If you look down at your toes and you're missing two rows,
That's a sure sign the toe-plucker's busy today.
Then what does he do when he's plucked quite a few?
He uses a toe truck to haul them away.

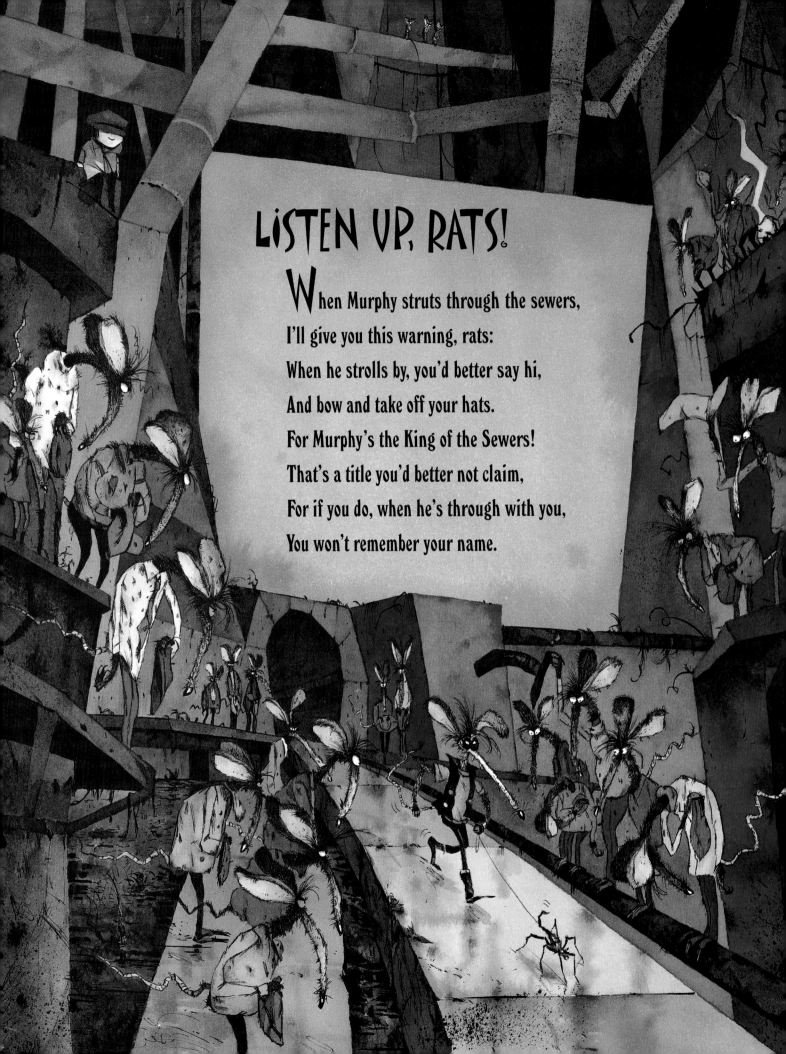

LISTEN UP, RATS!

When Murphy struts through the sewers,
I'll give you this warning, rats:
When he strolls by, you'd better say hi,
And bow and take off your hats.
For Murphy's the King of the Sewers!
That's a title you'd better not claim,
For if you do, when he's through with you,
You won't remember your name.

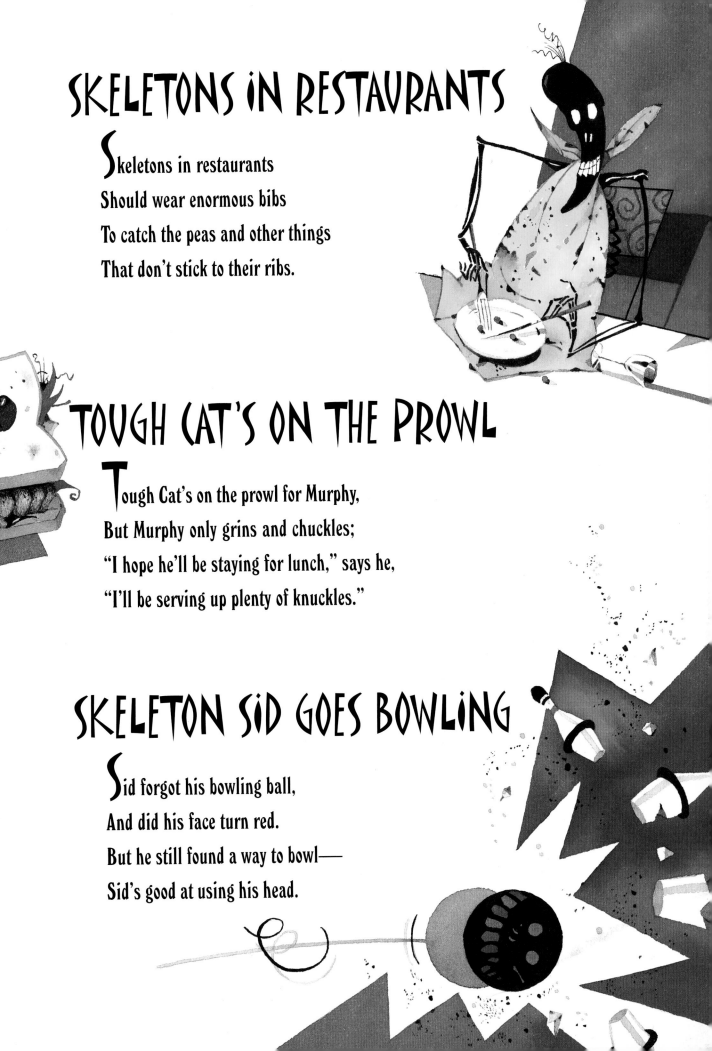

SKELETONS IN RESTAURANTS

Skeletons in restaurants
Should wear enormous bibs
To catch the peas and other things
That don't stick to their ribs.

TOUGH CAT'S ON THE PROWL

Tough Cat's on the prowl for Murphy,
But Murphy only grins and chuckles;
"I hope he'll be staying for lunch," says he,
"I'll be serving up plenty of knuckles."

SKELETON SID GOES BOWLING

Sid forgot his bowling ball,
And did his face turn red.
But he still found a way to bowl—
Sid's good at using his head.

JUDY

Judy has such lovely feet,
They reach halfway across the street.

TOMMY

Tommy tossed his two white mice
Into the washing machine.
And why, you ask, would he do that?
Why to make them squeaky clean.

THE EXAMINATION

Open your mouth, said the Doctor,
I want to examine your breath.
Well, it came out green and not very clean,
And choked the poor Doctor to death.

SAL HEARS A DRUMMING

Sal hears a drumming on her head
Every time it rains—
But stranger still is the sound up there
Whenever she uses her brains.

THE END OF TOMMY

Tommy chased the squirrels around,
He said it was such fun;
Until one day a squirrel went out
And bought a Tommy gun.

IF YOU EVER

If you ever stuffed cement
Into a hungry aardvark,
Its skin you could not scratch or dent,
For you would have a hardvark.

FRED

Fred said that bolts of lightning
Did not seem too fright'ning,
So one stormy night the dolt
Went outside and grabbed a bolt.
There was a clang and smoke and spark
And now our Fred glows in the dark.

GRANDMA

Grandma took her false teeth out
And set them on the chair;
When Gramps came in
He saw the chair grin,
And said, "Well, I declare."

ONE PORK AND BEAN

There sits my brother so serene—
But give him just one pork and bean,
And what he sits on, still and static,
Turns into a blast-o-matic.

ADVICE ON VAMPIRES

If some person you admire
Turns into a vampire,
Even though you may adore him,
Never stick your neck out for him.

A MUMMY WALKING IN THE CRYPT

A mummy walking in the crypt
Stepped on a banana peel and flipped
Over and over onto its head,
And it would have been killed—
If it hadn't been dead.

MURPHY IN DISGUISE

Who's that jingling Christmas bells?

Who's that wearing the reindeer hat?

Who's that leading a sleigh in the fog?

Why it's Rudolph the Red-Nosed Rat!

Paul Duggan is a poet, high school English teacher and librarian. His work has appeared in many anthologies, including *Till All the Stars Have Fallen* and *Here is a Poem*. *Two Skeletons on the Telephone* is his first book of poetry for children, and with it he hopes to revive the spirit and fun of Halloween year round

Daniel Sylvestre's work is found in films, magazines and even on wine labels. He studied Visual Arts in Montreal and in Paris and has illustrated over a dozen children's books, including the well-loved *Zunik* series. His diverse style and talents have earned him many awards and an international reputation as a children's book illustrator.